SPOTLIGHT ON TEXAS

Texas During Reconstruction

Greg Clinton

PowerKiDS press.

New York

Published in 2014 by The Rosen Publishing Group, Inc.
29 East 21st Street, New York, NY 10010

Book Design: Jonathan J. D'Rozario

Photo Credits: Cover http://en.wikipedia.org/wiki/File:Freedman_bureau_harpers_cartoon.jpg; p. 4 Fotosearch/Archive Photos/Getty Images; pp. 5, 11, 23 MPI/Archive Photos/Getty Images; p. 7 (Lincoln) Associated Press/AP Images; p. 7 (Johnson) http://en.wikipedia.org/wiki/File:President_Andrew_Johnson.jpg; p. 8 Courtesy of Library of Congress; p. 12 http://en.wikipedia.org/wiki/File:Edmund_Davis.jpg; p.13 Stephen Saks/Lonely Planet Images/Getty Images; p. 14 Courtesy of Library of Congresss; p. 15 Courtesy of Library of Congress; p. 16 Buyenlarge/Archive Photos/Getty Images; p. 17 Joseph Scherschel/Time & Life Pictures/Getty Images; p. 18 http://en.wikipedia.org/wiki/File:Freedmens_Bureau_1866.jpg; p. 19 http://en.wikipedia.org/wiki/File:Freedman_bureau_harpers_cartoon.jpg; pp. 20, 21 Peter Larsen/Getty Images Entertainment/Getty Images; p. 22 Courtesy of Library of Congress; p. 25 Hulton Archive/Archive Photos/Getty Images; p. 26 Erich Schlegel/Getty Images News/Getty Images; p. 27 Blanscape/Shutterstock.com; p. 29 (inset) Dallas Morning News/McClatchy-Tribune/Getty Images; p. 29 (main) AFP/Staff/AFP/Getty Images.

Library of Congress Cataloging-in-Publication Data

Clinton, Greg.
Texas during reconstruction / by Greg Clinton.
p. cm. — (Spotlight on Texas)
Includes index.
ISBN 978-1-4777-4518-2 (pbk.)
ISBN 978-1-4777-4519-9 (6-pack)
ISBN 978-1-4777-4517-5 (library binding)
1. Reconstruction (U.S. history, 1865-1877) — Texas. 2. Texas— Politics and government — 1865-1950. 3. Texas — Social conditions — 19th century. 4. Texas — Economic conditions — 19th century I. Title.
F391.C55 2014
976.4—dc23

Manufactured in the United States of America

CPSIA Compliance Information: Batch #WW14RC: For further information contact Rosen Publishing, New York, New York at 1-800-237-9932.

CONTENTS

THE CIVIL WAR AND RECONSTRUCTION

The American Civil War lasted from April 12, 1861, to April 19, 1865. In that time, more than 600,000 soldiers died in battle or from disease. More people were killed in the Civil War than in any other U.S. military conflict.

The Reconstruction era lasted from 1865 to 1877. During this time, the United States tried to rebuild its economy and restore national unity.

The Civil War was fought between states in the North, which wanted to abolish, or end, slavery, and states in the South, which used slaves to support their economy. The Northern states were called the Union, and the Southern states were called the Confederacy. After the Union won the war, the South was forced to make big changes. This period of U.S. history after the Civil War is called Reconstruction.

What Does It Mean to Secede?

In 1860 and 1861, many Southern states, including Texas, decided to form a separate country with a government that supported their beliefs and **culture**, which they felt were different from those of the North. They strongly believed in states' rights, especially as they applied to the issue of slavery, and felt the federal government had too much control.

Eleven states seceded, or broke away, from the United States by passing a law declaring they were no longer a part of the nation. They formed a new government called the Confederate States of America and elected their own president, Jefferson Davis.

Jefferson Davis

Early Reconstruction Plans

President Abraham Lincoln had already begun to develop a plan to readmit the Confederate states, including Texas, into the United States before the Civil War ended. He knew Reconstruction would not be easy because the Confederacy and the Union had spent four years fighting each other. It would take hard work to get both sides to come together to rebuild the nation.

When Lincoln was assassinated, or killed, on April 15, 1865, Vice President Andrew Johnson became president. Johnson's plan for Reconstruction called for forgiveness for anyone in a former Confederate state who took an **oath** of **loyalty** to the United States, but military officers and wealthy Southerners had to first ask the president for an official pardon. The states also had to accept the 13th Amendment to the U.S. Constitution, which called for the abolition of slavery in all states.

Abraham Lincoln

Andrew Johnson

Presidents Lincoln and Johnson both had to come up with plans for how to bring the Confederate states back into the nation after they seceded.

Unequal Citizens

Before the Civil War, many wealthy farmers owned not only land, but people—Africans who had been captured and forced to work in the United States against their will. By the time the Civil War began, slavery had been a major part of the Southern economy for over 200 years. When the 13th Amendment to the Constitution was passed in 1865, all slaves were freed. Many people throughout the United States believed former slaves should have the right to things such as **suffrage** and public education.

From the point of view of wealthy Southern farmers, this was terrible. Without slave labor, they would have to pay workers to raise crops, which would cost them money they never had to spend before. Many people in Texas were opposed to laws that would give former slaves freedom and rights. However, a smaller number of Texans wanted a better life for former slaves. The conflict between these two groups was an important part of the Reconstruction era in Texas.

When slavery ended in the South, many former slaves needed work, and many farms needed tending. Landowners set up a system called "sharecropping," which was very similar to the slave system before the Civil War. Poor black and white families participated in this system, but blacks were often bound by contracts that limited their movement and opportunities.

THE CONSTITUTION OF 1869

The federal government's first attempt to get the Texas government to accept the terms of Reconstruction wasn't successful. Many Texas politicians wanted to keep things the way they were before the Civil War, so it was hard for Reconstruction plans to work in the state. In 1867, the U.S. Congress passed Reconstruction Acts, which wiped out all the state governments in the South and replaced their leaders with new, handpicked ones. In other words, Congress forced the South to try to make Reconstruction plans work again, but this time with stronger leadership from the North.

Texans had to elect 90 male **delegates** to attend a constitutional convention between 1868 and 1869 to rewrite the state constitution. For the first time in Texas history, African Americans were included in the democratic process. They could vote in the election, and 10 of the delegates elected were African American. Even before the convention started, Texas democracy had changed in a big way, and it would continue to change after the creation of the Constitution of 1869.

African American men were fully included in the democratic process in 1870, when the 15th Amendment was passed, assuring them the right to vote.

A Stronger Government

The **Radical Republicans** who controlled Texas for the first years of Reconstruction wanted to create a strong central government. By giving broad power to the governor and Texas **legislature**, the Republicans, including Governor Edmund Davis, were determined to give African Americans equal rights. They felt African Americans should have a voice in government as well as access to legal protection and public education. Education was an important part of the Constitution of 1869. It created a statewide public school system funded by taxes. It also made school attendance required by law.

The Constitution of 1869 also gave Davis the ability to fill many state government positions with people who would support his ideas. Davis fought for the Union in the Civil War, even though he lived in Texas. That made him very unpopular in his state, and his increased powers as governor made many Texans like him even less.

Edmund Davis

Schoolhouses in Texas were filled with students thanks to the Constitution of 1869.

In addition to working for equal rights for African Americans, Davis created the state police to fight violence in Texas. This first police force included African American police officers, which made some Texans uneasy and made the state police unpopular. Davis was also responsible for creating a state **militia** to defend Texas, and this militia also included African American members. The state militia would one day become the Texas National Guard.

Davis's new ideas about how to help former slaves in Texas become full, productive citizens upset many white Texans. To them, black people were meant to remain beneath white people in society. Davis was so unpopular that he was voted out of office after only one term, which lasted four years. Although many Texans did not like Davis or the Constitution of 1869, both had a role in shaping modern Texas, especially its education system.

Governor Davis led many social reforms

He appointed new leaders who were friendly to the Republican cause.

He created the state police and Texas militia to help combat violence, especially against former slaves.

He set up new schools for former slaves and a new education system for Texas.

The state militia's job was to protect Texas from threats outside of the United States and to help state and local police forces if necessary.

Treatment of Former Slaves

While Davis was governor, he was committed to helping Texas's African American population. Unfortunately, some Southerners couldn't accept the rights former slaves were granted after the Civil War. Some of these Southerners responded with violence toward African Americans and anyone who supported their fight for equal rights. During this period, a **white supremacy** group called the Ku Klux Klan, also known as the KKK, was formed. Its members often used violence to scare African American communities in many states, including Texas. Violence against African Americans and their property soared in the years after the Civil War, and the Texas government didn't have the resources or support to stop it completely. For over a century, African Americans struggled to gain true equal rights and opportunities in Texas and throughout the South.

The fight for equality for African Americans in Texas continued for over 100 years after Reconstruction.

The Freedmen's Bureau

The U.S. Congress set up the Bureau of Refugees, Freedmen, and Abandoned Lands in 1865. This organization, also known as the Freedmen's Bureau, helped people who were left homeless by the Civil War and former slaves, known as "freedmen." The Freedmen's Bureau also paid attention to contracts that freedmen signed with white landowners to make sure the contracts were fair. For example, if there was a court case involving a freedman, the Freedmen's Bureau might step in if it felt justice wasn't being done. It also helped organize schools for African American children.

The Freedmen's Bureau hoped it could move Texas toward a fairer, safer, and more productive society with equal rights for all. It even tried to make sure freedmen were able to exercise their new voting rights in Texas and throughout the South.

The Freedmen's Bureau worked hard to make sure that the freedom former slaves won through the Civil War was protected.

The Freedmen's Bureau had trouble operating in Texas because of the state's large size and white landowners, who often resisted changes the bureau wanted to make. New laws passed by the Texas legislature, called "black codes," made life for freedmen very difficult. Many Texans believed the Freedmen's Bureau was just another part of the Northern army that was trying to force them to accept black equality.

Many of the bureau's agents were targets of violence, and by 1868, most of the bureau's projects were shut down. It did, however, continue organizing new schools for African American children. The Freedmen's Bureau ended its operations in Texas in 1870. However, the bureau made a lasting contribution to Texas's education system by increasing the number of African American children who had access to public schools.

The Freedmen's Bureau helped make sure that children of all races were able to get an education in Texas. That belief is reflected throughout Texas today.

An Ironclad Oath

After the Union won the Civil War, it wanted the former Confederate states to reform their governments. But because the United States was designed to be a **federation**, states had to make their own laws and constitutions instead of the federal government doing it for them. This meant that the same people who had fought against the North in the Civil War were now asked to make new laws that went against their beliefs.

The federal government realized this was going to be a problem, so they designed a way to exclude those leaders who were powerful before the Civil War. One of the new requirements for voting or being elected was making an oath that said you had never fought against the Union. This meant that thousands of Southerners who had participated in the war couldn't vote or run for office, allowing Radical Republicans to be elected instead. This "Ironclad Oath" made many people in Southern states, including Texas, furious.

Carpetbaggers and Scalawags

During Reconstruction, some Northerners traveled to the former Confederate states. Some of them wanted to purchase farms. Others wanted jobs rebuilding Southern railroads and buildings that had been destroyed during the war. Most Southern Democrats didn't like these Northerners, who they felt were trying to influence politics and destroy their way of life. They called Northerners carpetbaggers because it was said that they carried their belongings in a carpet sewed into a bag, which they wore over their shoulders.

Scalawags were almost worse. This is the name given to Southerners who agreed with the beliefs of the Union during the Civil War. Anyone from the South who supported Reconstruction reforms and the Radical Republican Party was called a scalawag.

During the Reconstruction era, this soldier would not have been able to vote or run for office because he fought against the Union.

The Constitution of 1876

By 1875, Reconstruction had been in place for 10 years. In that time, the federal government had done many things to force Southern states to change their laws, but it was very hard—if not impossible—to change people's attitudes. White supremacy groups even murdered black voters and Radical Republicans so that Democrats would win elections.

In 1873, a Democratic governor and a Democratic legislature took control in Texas. After being under the strong leadership of Radical Republicans, Democrats wanted to weaken the Texas government and replace the Constitution of 1869. Why did they believe this was a good idea? During Reconstruction, many former Confederates and white landowners felt the federal government was controlling their businesses and making them pay taxes to help poor black citizens. In their opinion, if the Texas government was weak, then it couldn't force rules on businesses, making it much harder to pass sweeping social reform laws.

The Democratic Party had power over Texas and other Southern states, known as the "Solid South," for the next century. The first U.S. president from Texas, Lyndon B. Johnson, was a Democrat.

The Constitution of 1876 began with a bill of rights, which stated that Texas was a free and independent state and subject only to the U.S. Constitution. It limited the power of the Texas government so that the governor had to share power with a number of elected officials. This is known as a plural **executive** branch of government. Also, the Texas legislature could only meet every two years.

Voters accepted the 1876 Constitution, and it's still in effect today. It has been amended hundreds of times, and it's more than 60,000 words long, making it one of the longest and most complex state constitutions in the United States. The authors of this constitution were afraid of a government that was too active and powerful. That's why the Constitution of 1876 set up a Texas government that's weak and small.

The Texas legislature meets every two years in the Capitol building in Austin.

The Effects of Reconstruction

The Civil War was a terrible time in American history, and the Reconstruction era in Texas was also very troubled. Southerners didn't like being forced back into the United States. Many of them also didn't like being forced to give former slaves freedom and basic rights. But while many historians look back at Reconstruction with mixed feelings, it set the stage for the civil rights struggles of the 20th century. It has taken a long time, but since then, African Americans have represented Texas in the U.S. Congress and have been elected as mayors of major cities, such as Houston and Dallas.

Reconstruction also helped create the Texas education system still in place today, as well as the constitution still used by the state. Even when Reconstruction was failing, brave and smart people worked hard to make positive changes in Texas that we can still see today.

Barbara Jordan was the first African American elected to the Texas senate after Reconstruction. She was able to serve her country because of the reforms made during the Reconstruction period.

Reader Response Projects

- Imagine you have traveled back in time to Texas during Reconstruction. Write a story about your life during this time period and how it's different from your life in modern times.

- Write an opinion essay in which you answer the questions: Was the North justified in trying to control the Reconstruction government of Texas? Why or why not?

- If you were a political leader in Texas during Reconstruction, what might you have done differently than the Radical Republicans? Write a plan with three main points.

- Create a poster that could have been used during Reconstruction to build support for the Freedmen's Bureau. Use details from the text and information from other sources to explain why the Freedmen's Bureau was important.

Glossary

culture (KUHL-chur) The beliefs and ways of life of a group of people.

delegate (DEH-lih-guht) A person with power to act for another.

executive (ihg-ZEH-kyuh-tihv) Of or relating to the carrying out of laws.

federation (feh-duh-RAY-shun) A group of states ruled by a central government but with each state keeping some independence.

legislature (LEH-jihs-lay-chur) An organized body of persons having the power to make laws.

loyalty (LOY-uhl-tee) The quality or state of being faithful.

militia (muh-LIH-shuh) A body of citizens with some military training who are called to be active only in an emergency.

oath (OHTH) A promise or sworn statement.

Radical Republican (RAA-dih-kuhl rih-PUH-blih-kuhn) A member of a branch of the Republican political party that developed before the Civil War and lasted until the end of Reconstruction. This branch was strongly opposed to slavery, distrustful of former Confederates, and in favor of granting civil and voting rights to African Americans.

suffrage (SUH-frihj) The right to vote.

white supremacy (WYT suh-PREH-muh-see) The belief that white people are better than people of any other race and should have control over society.

Index

Due to the changing nature of Internet links, the Rosen Publishing Group, Inc., has developed an online list of websites related to the subject of this book. This site is updated regularly. Please use this link to access the list: **http://www.powerkidslinks.com/sot/txrc/**